I0198820

The Grit and Joy of Being

The Grit
and Joy
of Being

Anne Poarch

BELLE ISLE BOOKS
www.belleislebooks.com

Copyright © 2020 by Anne Poarch

No part of this book may be reproduced in any form or by any electronic or mechanical means, or the facilitation thereof, including information storage and retrieval systems, without permission in writing from the publisher, except in the case of brief quotations published in articles and reviews. Any educational institution wishing to photocopy part or all of the work for classroom use, or individual researchers who would like to obtain permission to reprint the work for educational purposes, should contact the publisher.

ISBN: 978-1-947860-94-0

LCCN: 2019913512

Designed by Michael Hardison
Project managed by Christina Kann
Cover illustration by Sander Gibson, brother to the author
Author photo (pg. 73) by Tasha Tolliver via Palette Home

Printed in the United States of America

Published by
Belle Isle Books (an imprint of Brandylane Publishers, Inc.)
5 S. 1st Street
Richmond, Virginia 23219
belleislebooks.com | brandylanepublishers.com

BELLE ISLE BOOKS
www.belleislebooks.com

for Herbert and Peggy
Thank you . . .

"The Joy knows not of eroticism or materialism. That is temptation for itself. Joy came from and points in another direction. I, too, know this to be true. The Joy will remain. Temptations fade. Joy. Joy. Joy."
—Ruminations on C.S. Lewis, *Surprised by Joy*

"May I never not be frisky, May I never not be risque."
—Mary Oliver, *Evidence*

CONTENTS

Summer Epiphany

I like to call it summer epiphany.
Surprising discovery,
horses let out of the pen.

Monumental moment,
trotting first, then slowing to discover
        the freedom.
Freedom of a late afternoon breath
        and the caress of dragonflies' wings upon their knees.
A sigh of relief in feeling the stubble upon the earth
        under their lips.
To smell it with nostrils wide and heads pressing
the soft dirt beneath the scratchy surface of that ground.
Then rearing back, the surprising summer wind fully encircling
their bodies in that open field.
Wishing to kick off those shoes, bound as they were on their feet.

Sadly, the barn bell ringing, calling them back to the fence.
Shaking off the passion of life, a frustrated utterance escaping open mouths,
hanging heads leading them back to the pen.

Despite the stalls they would inhabit, their thoughts would
wander back to that day and others like it.
Roaming over the stubbly fields, through hidden valleys
and alongside fragrant streams.

Remembering the freedom of summer
and the epiphany that would carry their kinship
through fall, through winter, into the promise of a friendly spring.

Canopy of Gray

The snow is falling outside.
Early morning with only a breath of light,
if you can call the color gray light.
I would.
Shades of gray are where we so often find ourselves.
Neither black nor white,
Neither dark nor light.
Gray, as far as the eye can see,
can feel,
can touch.
Gray.
Ravens crest in that heavy sky.
A full, thick canopy of cloud,
sending out flakes.
Like a sieve, sifting confectioner's sugar across our world.
But I don't feel gray.
I feel light and love,
Despite the full thick canopy
spreading across my chest.

Liquid Spoon

Three cups of tea
was a good book.
Squeeze of lemon
Taste of honey
Hot liquid spoon
Stirring and stirring and stirring
        the pot
Until the heat of the Earl Grey
Finds the curves of my throat.
Taking on the shape of my body
Until I am fully the cup of tea
        myself,
Stirred and hot and sticky
                with honey.

Tongue-Tied

Tongue-tied and tentative,
tempered and tame.
Questions and comments,
carefully planned,

                        fall

like sand through an hourglass.
Drained from me
to rest at my feet,
weighing me down.
Arresting my full self
and keeping me on guard.
There was a timeless quality that day;
an ebb and flow of discourse,
a sweet, sweet shyness and uncertainty that,
while halted,
felt like easing into a summer's day.
A breath of warmth carried forth
from brighter days
and stolen moments of sunshine.
That the grains of truth and kernels of insight,
in which my feet were now buried
would drift away, was lost on me,
caught up in a wind
that crept through the back door.
A door that must have opened

when I closed the front door.
Left in shifting sand
my feet knew not
where to stand
and I fell.
But a great comfort I did not have far to fall;
thank goodness for those rooted trees that stand so tall.
So little time, so very, very little
Not enough to cover it all
Not enough to say what I was meant to say.

Dylan

Tonight I dreamed of you
        strumming your guitar
        on a patch of grass
        under a firelit sky,
        pops and rumbles in the
        distance.

Lighting the sky with bold and
        forceful proclamations,
        the display of light was a
        loud and bright counterpoint
        to your finger play on strings,
        pulling out a clear and dreamy
        strain.

While you strummed and the fireworks hummed,
        I caught it all . . .
        all of that summer night,
        intoxicating me through all of my senses:
        Sight, smell, sound, touch, taste.

I awoke with Dylan and the earth in my mouth.

The Gift

I feel strong and fearless.
Happy and content.
I love those breaths of summer.
The light.
The beauty.
The air that greets my skin.
The way I feel
and the way I see life
as the joy it is;
when I recognize the gift.
The precious gift.

Waiting

There's a tree swing
      with your name on it.
Under the moon.
Waiting for you.

Dolce Vita

I Wish My Words Were Snowflakes

I wish my words were snowflakes.
Bright and light and soft.
I'd like them to fall upon your ear
with quiet serenity,
drowning out the world,
dousing all fear.

I would like each flake to stand with meaning and purpose.
I want love to be their cloud.

Instead of harsh, sharp tones,
clipped or incessant talking
without thought, running on
so I leave you dry and parched.

I want instead to blanket your world in white.

Tuckahoe

Garden Club today at Tuckahoe Plantation, the home of my friend Sue. It is beauty. I've just returned to my car after taking a reflective tour of the grounds alone. So natural. So peaceful. I am feeling a tightness in my chest. A longing I cannot describe. Only to say as I walked through the garden, I felt an irresistible urge to strip naked. To take a handful of God's earth and smooth it all over my skin. Starting with my wrists, up my arms, across my bare chest, down my belly, up my legs. All over. I wanted to lie down in the clover and be one with the earth as a bridge to the sky. The birds and insects taking no notice of me. I am one with them and all of nature. I want to rub the dirt between my breasts and up my neck, into my hair. To pull the clover between my fingers and toes. To rest, alone, in beauty. To just be.

Girlie Girl

You make me want to be a girl.
      A girlie girl.
      Done-up toes,
      turning down rows and rows of dreams.
      Content to meander their verdant paths
      in summer song.

You make me want to be a girl.
      A girlie girl.
      Ribbons red,
      binding up those letters you'll send
      only to unbind and read again;
      the ribbon holding up my hair.

You make me want to be a girl.
      A girlie girl.

But here I am a woman.
      Drawn close to the fire,
      where ribbons burn red
      of an everlasting . . . desire.

Puzzle Piece

Fleeting beauty,
more than surface,
deeper than dreams.
Feel it all around;
the sound is silence.
The sound is you,
or is it me?
Imagine?
No, more real than day to day.
This is the puzzle.
How to keep the pieces in place
and not scattered across the floor.
Losing one piece under the rug,
ruins the whole. Find it. Right it.
No matter the fear.

One-Two Punch

Fantasy hits reality in a
one-two punch.
Or is it the other way around?
Probably so.
Reality is the aggressor.
Reality is the decider.
But what happens when part of that fantasy
is reality, too?
One-Two Punch!
In a second, I am knocked out cold.
Prone on the floor.
Dazed and confused.
Walking in a dream.
Drowning.
Clawing to find a way back to the fantasy,
but all eludes my grasp.
I keep coming up short.
Please, please; do not you see?
I am just asking for air,
For air to expand those lungs as far as they can possibly go.
To feel it, again.

Ebb Tide

Not even sure what I might like to write about.
Muddled head,
        tired spirit,
                waning joy.
Ebbs and flows,
It comes.
It goes.
This way in
and this way out,
on and on the roundabout . . .
we go.
Spinning slow, spinning fast,
fleeting moments will not last.
But to sustain them by the by,
lest we tell our heart . . . goodbye.

WOW

WOW ... No better words
     have ever been said.
WOW ... No proclamation
     so bold instead.
WOW ... Like music and
     song and surprise in one.
WOW ... Still mean it, day
     after day after day, is done.

Remembering Paul

Oh, he's still here.
I was just thinking of when
we were small.

When, in the backyard,
we would play
tetherball.

Closely wound,
then undone,
again and again the cycle's run.

Why cannot
we just stay wound close?
He is the one I miss the most.

Despite time, despite space
I love him
yet never get to see his face.

He, who is almost not there,
somehow pervades my everywhere.

Atlanta Airport

I see beauty on each face.
The tall and lanky man,
A worker.
Energy exudes from his pores, his being.
Shaved head; sunglasses perch on top
while cool, clear frames rest on the tip of his nose.
Beautiful, jangling chains flank the chest;
Bright eyes are aware.
They are music.
Music that matches the deep-set laugh lines
that crease his chestnut skin.

Of Being

I am fed up with convention.
I long to sit in the sand
            topless;
To be in the south of France
where wine with lunch
and showing skin
is a normal and everyday part
            of
                  being.

Not an arousal play.
Perhaps there is arousal but
in a purer form.
Aroused by life!
By senses!
By being!

I have this strange connection to the earth,
like I am one with the dirt and sand,
mud and clay.
Am I not formed from clay?

Leave me not in a box with artificial light.
Bring me out into the open,
baring skin, feeling a silken breeze,
tasting salt on my tongue,
hearing the clatter of cicadas and birds,
seeing blue sky and natural light,
smelling the hard brown earth.
And, on the wave of a summer wind,
salt, water, bark, leaves, and bougainvillea.
Smelling the essence
      of
          being.

Origami Heart

I knew it was time to pocket the memory.

Fold it up, ever so slowly, taking time to savor its beauty
        while carefully creasing each scene.

It was time to slide the origami heart between my fingers
        and let it rest for a moment in my palm,
        its intent wholly face-up.

Like sunshine pouring out, blinding me,
        reminding me of grace,
        reminding me to love and to give.

I tuck it deep inside the pocket of my skirt,
        pressed against my leg.

Touchable.

To give to others, not of self, but intentional giving,
        will lift the burden that fully opened memory
        has left upon my chest.

The sense of giving, the essence of love,
        will have to stay foremost on my mind when I reach
        to hold it between my thumb and index finger,
        rolling it around in my hand.

Because I am tempted . . . so, so tempted, with each selfless act
        to open it back up all the way,
        but it cannot be now, it is not time.

For now, it stays enfolded, no less palatable, in my heart.

Wash Away

I say I will let you wash away.
But, like the tide, you come back
again and again.
You crash on my chest
like a wave that pounds the surf.
The roar of the ocean,
that expanse of you,
echoes in my ear.
Pounding, pounding, pounding.
As the tide recedes and sunlight kisses the hard brown earth,
glistening, iridescent shells
fragmented and whole,
greet me as gifts.
A warm surrender to my heart and mind.
A calming refrain before the tide rushes back
to pound my chest again.

Probing

The butterfly was probing the lantana.
Bright summer blooms.
Dark magic butterfly.
Its flecks of blue and gold
against the tiny petals
of pink and yellow and orange.

Bittersweet passage of home.
Slender, white hands stroking piano chords.
Tear to eye, eye to sky, sky to flower bed . . .
       . . . the bed where the butterfly was weaving his summer dreams,
            the flutter of his summer symphony.

Dry

Dry, brittle, hard earth.
Green grass fades to straw in patches.
Withered leaves fall,
cracked and shriveled
       on the ground.
Like litter.
They shouldn't be there.
It is only July.
The air feels stiff and still,
as if outstretched arms, with palms flat,
would touch a wall of glass.
What I see and feel is too dry,
       too close to be real.
Stiflingly close, uncomfortably so.
Sky is white with a thick, moist haze
so I can barely
       breathe.
Feels like it will never change, always be this
hot, dry, thick, and sad.
But luckily . . . it will change.
Grass will green.
Skies will blue.
Air will clear.
Glass walls will fall, and there will be
       nothing
To stop those outstretched arms from running free
And hugging . . .
       every tree.

Remembering

I'd forgotten.

But today was a day when I remembered.

I took a walk in the early morning. First with my children and Maury.

Eager boys. Breath making smoke in the frosty air.

Then alone. But not alone. For you came back to me in that time.

The sun through the clouds as I cleaned your earth.

Past the Juniper with the blue berries I'd go back to pick later in the day.

To that sunny, bright, and happy spot. That fork in the road.

I'd forgotten.

But then, after the sun, after the spot, he mentioned Newton.

He mentioned grace. He mentioned "Amazing Grace" and I wept.

Almost two years ago he told the same story from the same pulpit.

A song to be sung. I remembered the connection to that song.

I'd forgotten.

But then at 10:39 am Karen Zacharias sent an email about her latest book.

I'd forgotten.

But Bet sold a hundred dollars' worth of shells from the James River.

I'd forgotten.

But then my boys and I played outside, cutting greenery for the house.

I'd forgotten.

But then we watched It's a Wonderful Life.

I'd forgotten.

But then I read Mary Oliver's "To Begin With, the Sweet Grass."

I remember.

I remember everything you wanted me to learn.

Tongue-Tied II

Tongue-tied and tentative, a bit maybe,
Still tempered but hardly tame.
Questions and comments,
more unsaid than said,
come this time as whispers at will,
edging on deep but circling around.
Enough talk to rustle the air
      with your voice,
      with my voice,
stirring up a sound as lovely as soft rain
or a dandelion floating on the air.
The melody of that tonal caress,
so right and soft in my ear,
like a fragrant wind circling my head
      to end in a smile.
Always a smile, quite a bit absent before,
so a joy and a treasure to see on you
and feel within as the corners of my mouth
      find their way up and up.
Up on the lilting music of what was stirring in that room.
Enough talk to rustle the air, to rustle my skirt,
but not so much to cover the comfort of the silence.
Easing right on back into that summer's day,
enveloping me again in its heady scent.
A quiet comfort.
A prelude to tea.
To sit and smile and
Just be.

Sea Foam

I am so tired of being sad.
Of those tears.
Of my emotions
that seem to rest just under the surface
      of my skin.
It feels like an ocean of salty tears
lazes behind my eyes
and what brings them forth
is the thought
      of a beauty.
A beauty I cannot touch or access.
I'm allowed to hold it in my mind
but not
      to feel

      or taste

      or even see.
This elusive love that floats on the sea like foam.
There is more and more of it from the source
but when touched, it
      dissipates

      away

      on the shore.

Spinning Out

The grief spins out
like gravel under tires
wheeling to get away.

To get away from the pain
of missing so much
missing my heart
as amplified by you.

I can't drive fast enough
or smart enough
or far enough
to get away from the sweet
sweet memory of you.

And tears come hard
like rain on the dirt road
pounding and pounding and pounding
until they slow
and the wheels
stop spinning
pulling up
to rest under the embrace of a tree.

Final drops of rain
drip and drip into
slow puddles of a soul
that aches and aches
for itself
as it swims in the grief—of you.

M Street

See the dog
        crawling down M Street,
Searching the sidewalk
        for something.
Sniffing skirts,
Looking for the one
The fringed felt one,
        falling from the bee's knees.
Like a wandering waterfall
        the fringe is a wall to
        hidden hills and those
        yet-to-be-explored caves.
He is all nose and knees himself,
        craning, wanting, hopeful,
        loyal to his quest.

In a flash of furious feet
        the canine is caught up
        in the clamoring crowds,
        swept into the tube.
Dazed by the bright bulbs of florescence
        and crushed close,
        the wrong sorts of sweat and salt
        mingle about his muzzle.

He pants, his racing heart beginning to slow
  as he sits quite still
  knowing he's lost the true scent,
  his true salvation.
Recalling the taste on his tongue,
  licking his lips as if to catch a last moment
  lingering in the light.
He pants again. Waiting until released from metal doors
  and free to search again.
Sniffing skirts to find
  his native one.
  His master. His home.

Stinging

How did the sun
        peeking through the clouds
        draw the sting behind
        my eyes?

In one moment, I am pretending
        I'm on top of the world,
        all figured out.

But then the sunlight,
        the song in the air,
        and I am sad
        for the beauty.

The beauty I still cannot touch,
        or feel, or taste, or see,
        or be.

Six Poems

I sat on the beach early this morning,
        feeling the wind blowing,
        as steady as surfsong.

And I wrote at least six poems in my head:
the dark cloud, the sand crab, the patient heron,
the frogman, the sweet dog that came to my side.
        My hand found itself buried
        in the thick, coarse coat of black fur.
        His dark eyes turned to me
        glints of gold reflecting in that morning sun
        before he took off to roll my scent in the sand.

And then, the one where you are in them all:
        the eyes of the dog, the skitter of the crab,
        the stare of the heron, the hop of the frog,
        even the dark cloud to the right of the sun.

Artistry

Artistry, it was your artistry
that brought the color to my cheeks,
the song into my soul.

Like the rose glow of early morning,
calling out from my eastern window,
calming my restless soul.

A balm to all that ails.
A return to the tales of tinted lips,
telling truths only the wild things comprehend.

Blooming, even now, still blooming inside of me.
A rose of ruby red bursting within,
revealing upon my face a blush of untold origin.

Artistry, it was your artistry
that brought the color to my cheeks,
the song into my soul.

Reindeer Lights

Dancing through reindeer lights,
like little flashes of light themselves.
In the cool, cool, crisp,
dark night air.
Running like the wind,
only to circle back again.
Whizzing by.
What must it have felt like to be them,
my boys, eye level with the lights,
surrounded by the white beams of Christmas
as they ran,
arms outstretched,
not one bit cold,
just carefree.

Red River Run

2012 first prize for Lyrics to a Song, Poetry Society of Virginia Contest

River rolling swiftly by
Roots me to this place.
Where would I be now
If I'd never seen your face?

Breast of robin beats in May,
Throbbing red for me.
Throats her tune in time
To when you and I were we
And the river ran free.

Chorus
Red River Run, won't you run right through my veins?
Let your ruby lips like a rose bloom in my soul.
Let the cool refrain of that river's reign.
Wash down over me as the river stakes its claim.
Red River Run, Red River Run.

Holding hands, we hoped to find
A slow and gentler pace,
To live a life worthwhile,
Defined by grace.

Let your talker, taster,
Devour the blooming buds,
Taking in the sweetness
Of that river's love.
You were a gift from above.

Chorus

Red River Run, won't you run right through my veins?

Let your ruby lips like a rose bloom in my soul.

Let the cool refrain of that river's reign.

Wash down over me as the river stakes its claim.

Red River Run, Red River Run.

Red River Run, won't you run right through my veins?

Take a walk with me,

Right down by the stream.

We could rest for hours,

Feeding on our dreams.

Let our tawny toes

Dip into the flow.

Mine like painted petals

Of the blooming rose will show.

But no one will know.

Chorus

Red River Run, won't you run right through my veins?

Let your ruby lips like a rose bloom in my soul.

Let the cool refrain of that river's reign.

Wash down over me as the river stakes its claim.

Red River Run, Red River Run. (River)

Red River Run, Red River Run. (Won't You?)

Red River Run, won't you run right through my veins?

Northwind

Last Tuesday, mosquitoes
feasted on my bare and tender skin.
Ankles, the tops of my feet, were like
pincushions for their stings.
But I didn't care.
I let the salty surf caress the growing welts
while the moonlight bathed my face
in its luminous glow.
Cool, foamy water lapped at my skin
in easy, fluid strokes while I waited
for the call of the wind.
And in it blew, with assurance and the
warmth of all my very best
summer days.
It came up behind me as I stared out
across the wide, expansive sea.
Behind me, the touch of that wind
stirred my hair while enveloping me
in a sure and sultry embrace.
It held me there, wrapping around my arms
and pressing against my back and thighs,
this strong sensation blowing in from the north.
And the wind stayed on that beach,
supporting my weight, taking on the shape
of my body.
I rested in that moment with a fullness of conscious
that took me with comfort and serenity into a place
so real, so present, all else faded from thought.
Forgetting, too, the wind would have to soldier on,

blowing down to other coasts in time.
But oh, I have never known a wind to feel so good,
so much like going home.

This Tuesday, I awoke to ankles itching with renewed vigor,
even though I had not been near any mosquitoes.
Surreal it seemed.
Were they just itching for the surf,
for the wind . . .
Or were they, in fact, itching
for home.

Snippets

Snippets of delusion.
Snippets of delight.
Remain not a dream,
But time standing still,
Fixed, locked, decidedly there.
To have a snippet is to linger.
To linger is to love.
To love is no delusion,
Only pure delight.

Pain

It is painful sometimes
like a knife.
The tears squeeze out
as the knife wields
its power.
Then release . . . and the pain becomes
bearable, and then turns to a
thankful joy.
The tears turn to salt on my hands.

Sycamore

The sycamore sheds her bark
like I slough off the old me.
In pieces it falls.
Sometimes large strips find their way
to the ground and at
other times little bits are
blown by the wind.
Collected at my feet are the vestiges
of that old and tired self.
Who will clean it up?
Who will take the pieces home and
paint pictures on them?

Sycamore II

The wind thrashed and blew
two nights ago.
In its wake, so many downed limbs and branches.
Even whole trees.
I saw one today.
A sycamore
On St. Andrews Lane
At least sixty feet tall—
felled.
I was so saddened.
Its white bark shining like gold in the early morning light.
The flecks of gray and taupe,
the green leaves resting
on the ground.
I felt tears well up behind my eyes.
I wanted to run to it.
I wanted to hug it.
I wanted to kiss it,
to stroke its smooth, creamy skin,
and whisper it,
goodbye . . .

Rookery Days

Rookery days,
Skipping stones.
Making love,
lips were sewn
together
like soft petals fall
before the seeds were thrown
into a sacred wall
of earth and deed,
truth and need.
A ground no longer
encumbered
by confines of her orb,
but open to new flights
and heady heights
to soar, wings wide
once more.

Petal Soft

I watch a red leaf
fall quietly
      to the gray asphalt road.

Simple sensation,
I felt it in my chest,
      like your petal soft lips upon my breast.

Red Leaf

I'm finally weaving it together.

The disparate threads of my life.

The myriad colors that have been blowing in the wind.

Driven by whims and dreams and loves. Desires running deep, the base color holds forth the form and will not let all the other colors drop. Cormorant on the water. Picking at his chest. Spreading dark wings, feet planted on firm rock surrounded on all sides by water. You can do and be anything you want to be; you dream to be Margaret Anne.

A teaspoon in the grass by the path to the river.

My tears taste like your skin.

Walking on larger path now, but sunlight and a fleck of gray-blue out of the corner of my eye, and a great blue heron takes off from a grouping of rocks by the shore. I walk there, and they are familiar rocks that bring a smile. The boys, swimming. Mavis, photo shoot. I watch the heron fly to a mate halfway across the river. Then, sitting on rock where we took John Quincy the frog, feeling the sun beat down, the water lap the shore, listening to "Home" by Dara Maclean, I had a flood of memories pre-six. Hermitage Road. Some I didn't know I had. Of Daddy, of the house. Of me, sitting alone in quiet places, contemplating. The roof off Mom and Dad's bedroom, my playhouse, the laundry room, the living room window with white curtains, under the stairs, the den, the field. So this is who I've been all along. I need quiet reflection.

And walking out on rocks, birds calling, I found another butterfly bush.

I took a photo——and left it there.

Then walking further, a green Dasani bottle cap.

On my way back, a few red leaves littering the path.

Look, Mommy! Red leaf! Red leaf, Mommy! Red leaf!

Ripening

Strawberries ripen
blond sunrise
into a life lived well
            and happy
falling off the table
landing south of me
            and east
calling to the sea
a new freedom
windblown hair falling from a braid
to release those long locks
lucky to have the caress of a father
when waiting lips call her home

Most of All

There goes the blur,
the whir of memories,
Flashes of color:
Midnight blue, deep purple,

Scarlet red, soft lavender gingham, golden honey, pink seersucker, bright eye popping yellow, teal teal teal, palest of blue, earl grey, colonial green, and white. Most of all, white. Most of all. Most of all, white . . .

The Pathway

It felt like the pathway
Halfway to the lodge.
In summer,
We found a little bridge
To cross
Where dragonflies kiss
The weathered wood
Softened from years of rain,
A bird trilling out a sound
Like passion or fear or warning,
The closeness of the morning
So close and deep and quiet
but for the birds and the crickets and other early summer sounds.
Sounds like murmurs and hushed tones and the long train
that came before.
If the train had come along after the bridge,
we might have chased it, hoping for a handhold.
Two runaways hiding from the world. Hiding from everyone
but each other.

The Dawn

The beauty of the morning in St. Pete. The dawn. The moon with the orange ring around it. The story of creation and us as stewards. The sky. The bright star. The water. Yoga. Walk. Run. Pray. Praise, creation. The heron that flew into my path so close I could touch. Plumb . . .

Tiger's Tail

You are my tiger's tail
Last grasp at truth
Constellations swimming
Grabbing for all my worth
              the essence
                    of the Milky Way
The moonlight waits for no one
Even us.

To Be

Soft skin, creamy light,
Dragonfly kiss,
The bridge of sighs
Tapered down to just a
Couple of kids
True friends lost
in a summer morning,
wanting only
To be
And to have the time to be it.

Ode to Life
(as told from a single peony)

I

Enclosed in a bud
        a tight-fisted peony, multi-petaled
Fighting the clenching embryo
        from within.
The right amount of sun
        and rain
        and ants
Climbing and sucking
        opens the petals one by one.
The fullness
        expanding with fragrance
        releasing me to the light and air
Flinging me out
            into the wide world.

It was all mine, this beautiful, passionate, sensual world
        with her light and her colors,
        her silken skies turned to the very
        best sort of playground for my wandering eye.
Flung out to try, flung out to fly
        anywhere and everywhere I wanted to go.
My oyster of promise,
        briny earth that tasted like heaven
                and tempted like hell.

II

And the temptation teased one too many times,
with no resolution, no completion
and I went flying back to the stem.
Looking for safety that wasn't really there.
Crawling past the spent stamen to an empty pistil,
        letting petals droop in on me
                      one by one.
Encased and alone.
Craving still those moments of light and life.
Wishing again to have been happy with just the temptation.
To cry out oh, oh, oh again with reckless abandon.

III

Then the gardener came with patient, practiced hands,
Cutting the stem to fall in a pile,
Last petals falling off, carpel nestling between blades of grass
        attending an assured toss in the rubbish bin.
But wait! Tender hand of the steward, kneeling in the grass
Fingers caressing leathery cases
Cracking open their promise,
        there with me all along
           still bent on creating something new and beautiful,
Life.

Dandelion

Have you ever seen a man pick a flower?
Stooping with unabashed joy at seeing a yellow sprite
saluting from the side of the road.
Fingers plucking it, a smile taking over his face as he breathes it in.
Pulling in the scent of the earth and a fragrance reminiscent of his
childhood,
of lazier days tromping through fields that stretched like dreams dotted
yellow along the river,
or languishing in the shade of a summer backyard, watching his sister make
dandelion chains.
Dandies under your chin, Brother! See there?
Do you like butter? butter butter butter butter butter
Do you like butter?
Neck smeared golden, see Mom? I like butter!
extra butter for my bread please, Mom.
A crown of dandelions cast him the king.
He breathes it in, his childhood and his luscious present,
found while simply out for an innocent morning run.
Have you ever seen a grown man, with unabashed joy, pick a flower?

Embraced

Enshrouded in white for a minute—
no, less.
It was less than that,
but it contained my world.
Pulling those ribs over my head,
Revealing skin, white sheathed all around,
Embraced by the cage of you.

A Morning Poem for You

The moonlight falls
right on top
      of the attic roof
this early, early September morning.

Cascading down blue slate
like water falls
      or velvet spills
to puddle at my feet.

I want to walk on that moonshine
to rise higher, like that slate
      prized from the earth
solid stones in the sky.

Golden Globes

The sun rises
    and it was good.
The moon returns
    and it was good.
The dance of a day
      between
The breath of a night
      to dream
The earth to hold
      our needs
Her ground is ours
      to keep
Sacred.
This spinning orb goes 'round
      so fast
But seems quite still beneath
      the grass.
With nature stirring goodness
      down below her soil
Abundance comes from God
      not man's ceaseless toil.
Simply part the veil
      of her planetary robes
In Honor.
And there arise those magnificent
      golden globes
That give us place to play
And provide much needed rest.

Ode to a Birthday

Oh you.
This day circles again into view
and slips so easily onto my frame.
Like a sure sweater or a favorite sock
gliding onto my touchpoint to the world.
This day arrests me—
the sun sliding onto my hands
like a gentle glove,
stopping the dark,
perfectly caressing awareness.
Asking of me only to walk,
side by side, this day with her,
hand in hand
through her shining depth.
Interlacing fingers,
touching palms
for a walk down a woodland path
maybe to the river,
or maybe to that autumn place
that continues to circle us forward
into promise and back into memory.
Heavenly Blessings Descend!
Happy Birthday Again!

Shoelaces

I gave up
       and I gave in
       To conformity
       To what was expected.
And what did I gain?
A weakened view of the world.
A hazy forecast and tireless troubles.
That which I thought would keep me upright
       (righteousness, no?)
dragged me down, centering my soul in my heels
       instead of my heart.
In my heels, where I would step on my own darling beauty
       that superb spirit I left dangling like an untied shoelace
              dragging in the dirt.

Lunch Outside

I just had lunch outside.

Trees . . .air satin . . . birds singing sweetly . . . breeze floating flower petals . . . lawnmower humming in the distance . . . church bells chime one o'clock nearby . . . bees lighting on my lavender . . . weeding to be done . . . it will wait . . . blue sky . . . bare feet.

I just had lunch outside.

I was thinking of you.

She and Tea

She came for tea.

Now, I am standing at the sink,
        hot water running from the faucet,
        glancing out the western window.
Soapy suds fill the sponge
and find the bright hue of her lipstick.

I think of her smile and her ease
        and our friendship.
A warmth spreads like the setting winter sun,
        soft light tucked behind the trees,
        the rose glow shining through.
I remember the talk and the tea
as the sponge clears away
        her ruby lips.

Then, in an instant,
        gone.
Gone is the trace of the hot pink kiss
        from the cup,
        from the sky.
Lasting is the warmth and the smile.

Goldfinch II

The goldfinch was looking for her mate.
Lilting through the dying fig tree
her hurried hop was frantic as she danced
from lonely limb to lonely limb.

Looking.
For where was his sunlit body?
His harp of a voice?
Bright yellow sprite
who gave her days of dandelion dreams?
Where was his daring, melodious throat
that held her heart?

She longed for that sound, that sweet song;
such harmony heightening
when they sang together.
But the day was waning and gray
so she left the barren fig
and continued her search elsewhere.

A cardinal followed her.
Protection? A Sign?

I was so sad for her.
I wanted her to hear again
his call to her alone
from the depths of a bush and his soul.

I longed for them to fly together.

Turning to the tangled yard
and finding solace in clipping ajuga and clover,
those flowers of my childhood.
Squatting low to the carpet of age-old common blooms,
royally there shown a four-leaf clover,
unafraid, not hiding, but seen.

Luck for the finch's quest?

Fiuymi
(fake it until you make it)

I feigned the joy.
Pretended the smile.
Drew up the laugh from some burning place within
that knows the truth.

I kept it up,
this happy mirage,
until, like dew,
droplets of joy settled on my heart.

As the moisture seeped in
the smile began to appear,
unannounced,
and as it did
the droplets of joy
began to grow and patter like steady rain.
After sustained practice,
I found myself joyful again,
sitting on my screened porch listening to the summer rain
now sprinkling my heart.

Interpretation, please?

i sat with you that long-awaited hour
        together
stones falling underfoot while my hand held firm
to the hard, flat surface, taut line to the truth
that was disappearing as floods came and took away my footing
and you screamed out my name for fear
        you'd lost me
again in the mist of time and too much stuff
that we bent our heads in sadness knowing we might miss the shore
but the roots were there, and we held on together
        or i held on to you
that leather cord of remembrance,
and i climbed to the top of the tree to see our way into a new land
of fertile shores and open skies.

Living Water

The grief sits
like a stagnant pond,
neither moving through anything
nor to anywhere.

Her heart is clogged in the chorus
        of the repeated refrain.
She keeps coming along and filling new holes,
        new breaks with mud
for fear the long-held reverie of punctured sadness
will subside, whither, retreat into a well so deep
the beauty it contains will be no more.

Through her rose-colored glasses, her ardent lens,
the pond is peaceful and permanent.

To others
        who live in the present
        or their own cloistered truth
        it is sullen and murky.
Damned.
Blocked from the flow of living water.

Finally, one day, her eyes will open and see as it is,
        the herons had stopped their fishing,
        the songbirds stopped their nesting,
        dragonflies stopped their molting,
and she will no longer see it as fresh
but will smell the rot of decay.

Thus resolved,
        the leaves and the muck
        will be cleared.

The earth moved to its rightful place
　　　　for the water to run free.

The damn will break in a
　　　　final flood
　　　　　　　of sorrow
washing over her desperate, changed soul
　　　　to wash it clean.

Years hence, looking back
　　　　upon that grief of a pool
will be but memory
　　　　of all that came before what stands before her now;
a pleasant stream of living water where birds chirp and tadpoles swim.
The earthy fragrance of moss and a clean spirit in the air
　　　　where a goodly brook points the way.

To life.

Kittens

They long to bathe the kittens. I long to sit and write.

Grit & Joy

There is grit and joy in life.
You can eat a peach,
taste the soft silky sweetness of the fruit,
and still catch a flake of pit in your mouth.
I'll take the unwelcome to get at the heart.
Come and visit the orchard with me;
We'll shake the trees and give out bushels of joy.

"And what do I risk to tell you this, which is all I know? Love yourself. Then forget it. Then, love the world."

—Mary Oliver, *Evidence*

"I believe that the old stab, the old bittersweet, has come to me as often and as sharply since my conversion as at any time of my life whatever. But I now know that the experience, was valuable only as a pointer to something other and outer."

—C.S. Lewis, *Surprised by Joy*, Chapter XV

Don't Leave

I caught a leaf dancing there
out of the corner of my eye
In that bright and happy spot
I often happen by
It turned and danced
and beckoned me
Come stay a while and dance...
you'll see

You'll see the sun.
You'll see the rain.
You'll see laughter
and you will see pain.
But know inside, deep down inside,
that what you see, in fact, is me.

Surrounded

Shadows fall away
      like some slow fade,
      dissolving like water imbibed
          by thirsty soil.

Finding cracks,
      liquid longings
      spill, seep, and lose
          their permanence.

The seamless dark is gone,
      careened off a cliff,
      leaving only open sky
          and light bursting forth

              from the heart.

About the Poet

Anne Poarch grew up the youngest of five children in the Sandhills of North Carolina. Always mindful of her roots, Anne's early childhood experiences with nature and family helped inform her path to poet and entrepreneur. After graduating *cum laude* from Wake Forest University in 1991, Anne traveled to Paris, where she worked as an *au pair* for the Picasso family and attended the University of Paris, Sorbonne. After her year-long sojourn abroad, she returned to live and work in Richmond, Virginia, where she lives today with her husband and two sons. Anne gathers inspiration for her poems from touchpoints in nature that represent the ephemeral connections of life and beauty. The same calling from which the poet emerged inspired the creator in Anne to leave a twenty-two-year career in the financial services industry to seek a deeper connection to the beauty, spirit, and joy in natural life. Anne is the founder of Basket & Bike, a bicycle tour company that promotes leisurely excursions in nature. Through her business and her poetry, Anne empowers people to connect with the land and their communities in graceful, new ways. Basket & Bike gives back a portion of every tour to conservation causes in the Richmond area. *The Grit & Joy of Being* is her second book of poetry. Her first book, *Flight: of butterflies and robins and other winged dreams*, was published in 2017.

www.ingramcontent.com/pod-product-compliance
Lightning Source LLC
Chambersburg PA
CBHW020455100426
42813CB00031B/3378/J

* 9 7 8 1 9 4 7 8 6 0 9 4 0 *